The Official
RONNIE AND NANCY
Cat Book

The Official RONNIE AND NANCY Cat Book

by BILL ADLER
with photographs by
SUZANNE SZASZ

QUILL
New York 1981

Copyright © 1981 by Bill Adler and Suzanne Szasz

Nine of the photos appearing in this book are reproduced from *The Silent Miaow* by Paul Gallico, picture story by Suzanne Szasz. Copyright © 1964 by Paul W. Gallico and Suzanne Szasz. By permission of Crown Publishers, Inc.

All rights reserved. No part of this book may be reproduced or utilized in any form or by any means, electronic or mechanical, including photocopying, recording or by any information storage and retrieval system, without permission in writing from the Publisher. Inquiries should be addressed to William Morrow and Company, Inc., 105 Madison Avenue, New York, N.Y. 10016.

Library of Congress Catalog Card Number: 81-85063
ISBN 0-688-01187-X (pbk.)

Printed in the United States of America

First Quill Edition

1 2 3 4 5 6 7 8 9 10

DESIGNED BY BERNARD SCHLEIFER

PERSONAL NOTE

This book was written in good spirit and hopefully in good humor and certainly with great respect and affection for President and Mrs. Reagan—and for that wonderful, warm creature called the cat.

Bill Adler
New York City

I think Al Haig wants to see the President again.

I don't care if it is 60 Minutes—no cameras are allowed in the Lincoln Bedroom.

But, Ronnie, isn't there anything left for the Democrats?

I'm not letting you up, Tip, until you pass our program.

William Safire's column is fascinating.

I know Jimmy left some peanuts around here somewhere.

The CIA is on top of the case, Mr. President.

Once a day Ronnie lets me sit in his chair in the Oval Office.

Another Republican fund-raising dinner

I've been Mrs. Reagan's hairdresser for two years.

Maybe we should put in real plumbing at the ranch, Ronnie.

Kissinger's not leaving until the President gives him a foreign assignment.

Who took the President's horse?

Mr. President, what are you going to do for the farmers?

How am I ever supposed to get finished reading the federal budget?

I'm really glad I married you.

Mirror, mirror, on the wall, who is the fairest First Lady of them all?

The Moral Majority is just going to die when they see this.

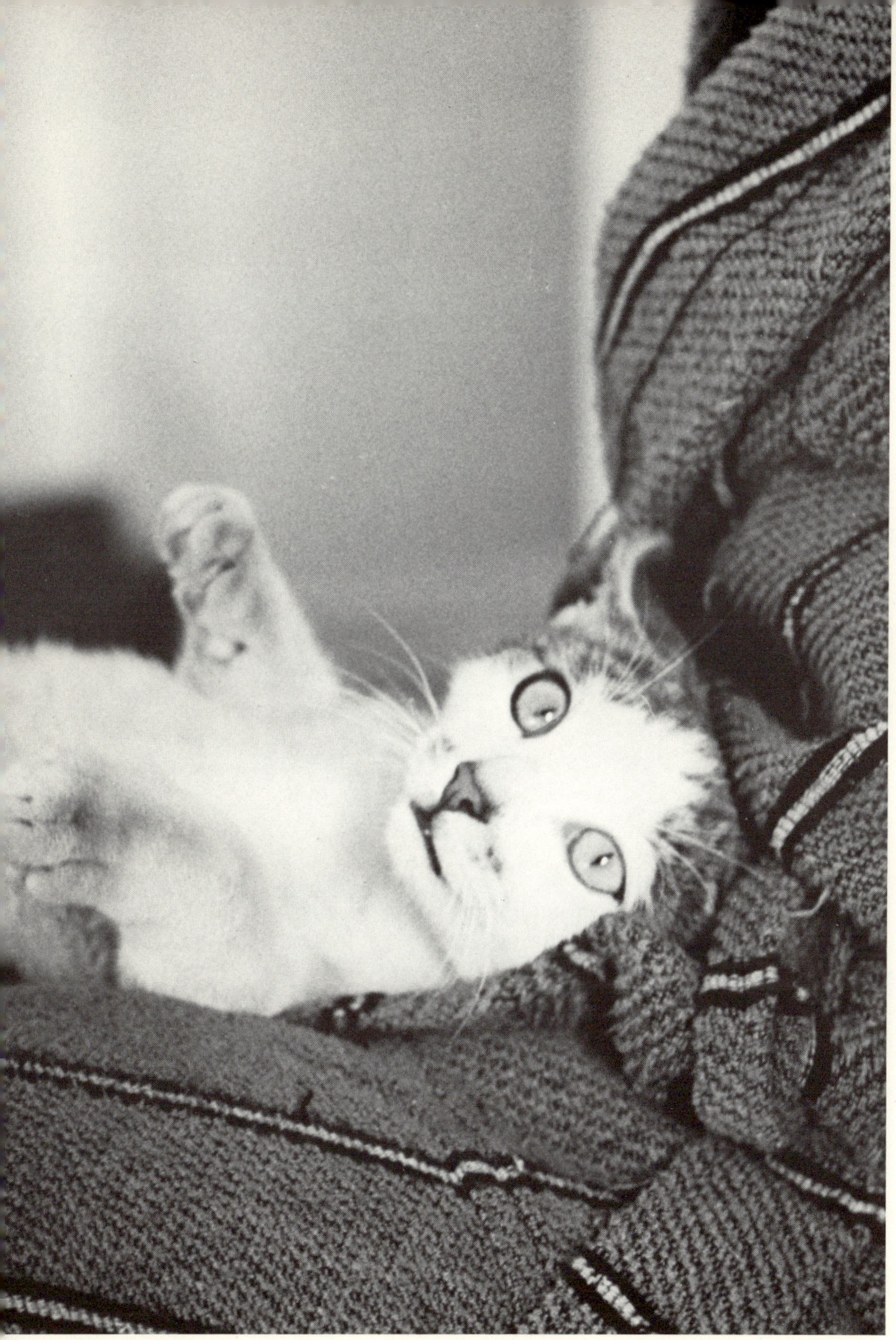

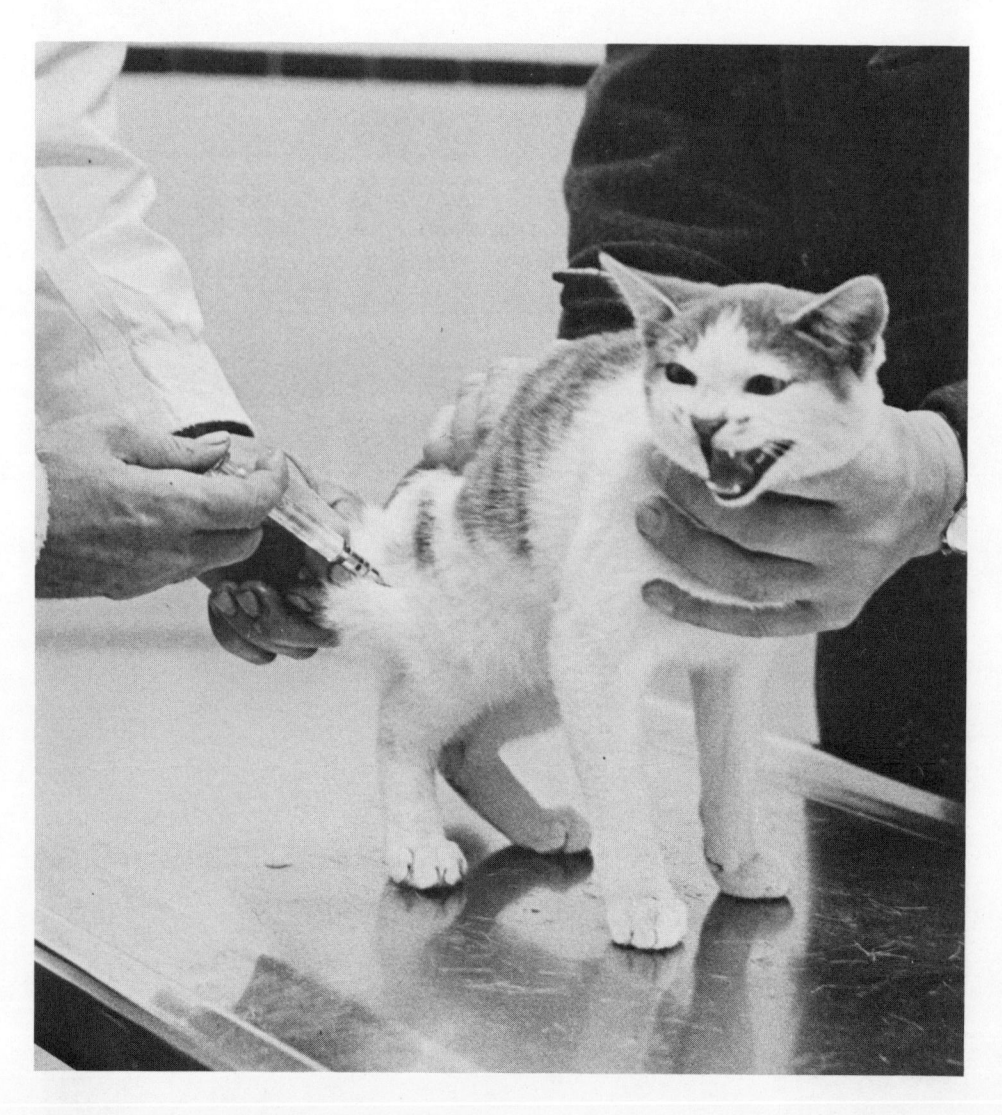

Are you sure Medicare still takes care of this?

I wish we didn't have to go so far for these summit conferences.

We're Deaver, Meese, and Baker—special assistants to the President.

I'm not going downstairs until the band starts "Hail to the Chief."

Nancy, how long does it take to get dressed for a state dinner?

Ronnie. It's me—Jimmy. Could Rosalynn and I have just one more look around?

Listen, Maureen, just wait. Someday you will be a senator.

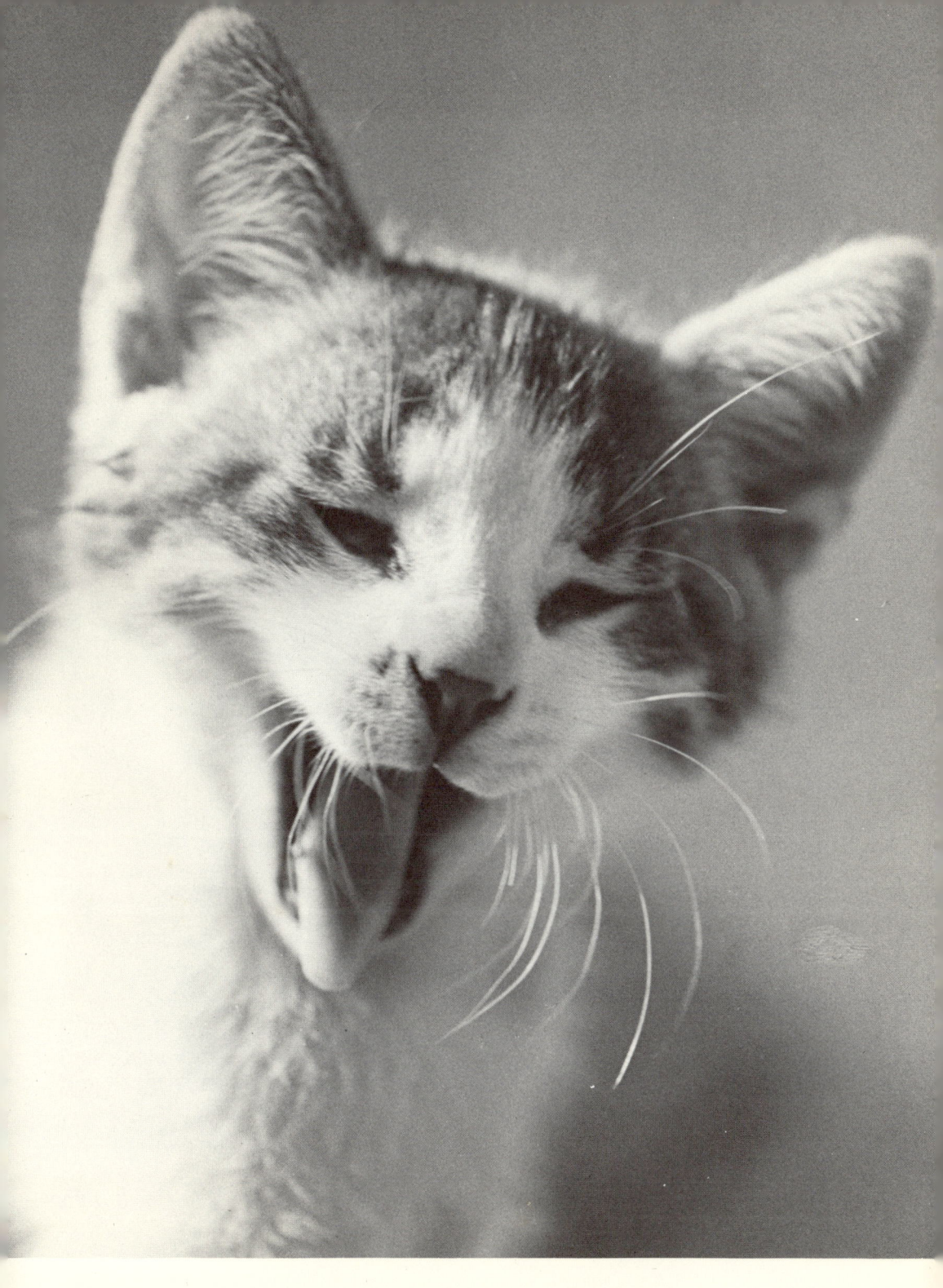

Time *magazine is going to make me Man of the Year.*

I don't care if Brezhnev is on the hot line. Can't you see I'm busy?

How come Al Haig gets his own chair at the Cabinet meetings?

Ronnie keeps me on a pedestal.

Anytime you want, Mr. President, we're ready to start the Cabinet meeting.

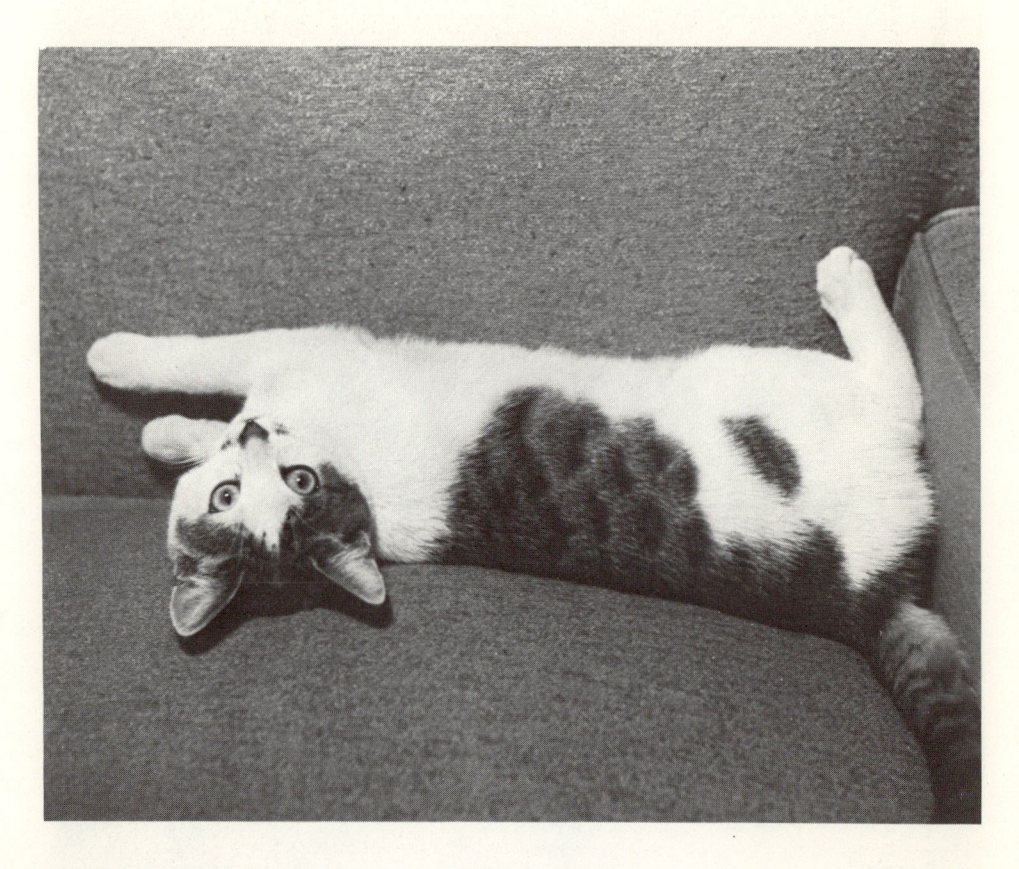

Gosh, Mr. President, you really are tall!

Really, Mr. President, you *were* once a Democrat.

Don't you think we should work this out in caucus?

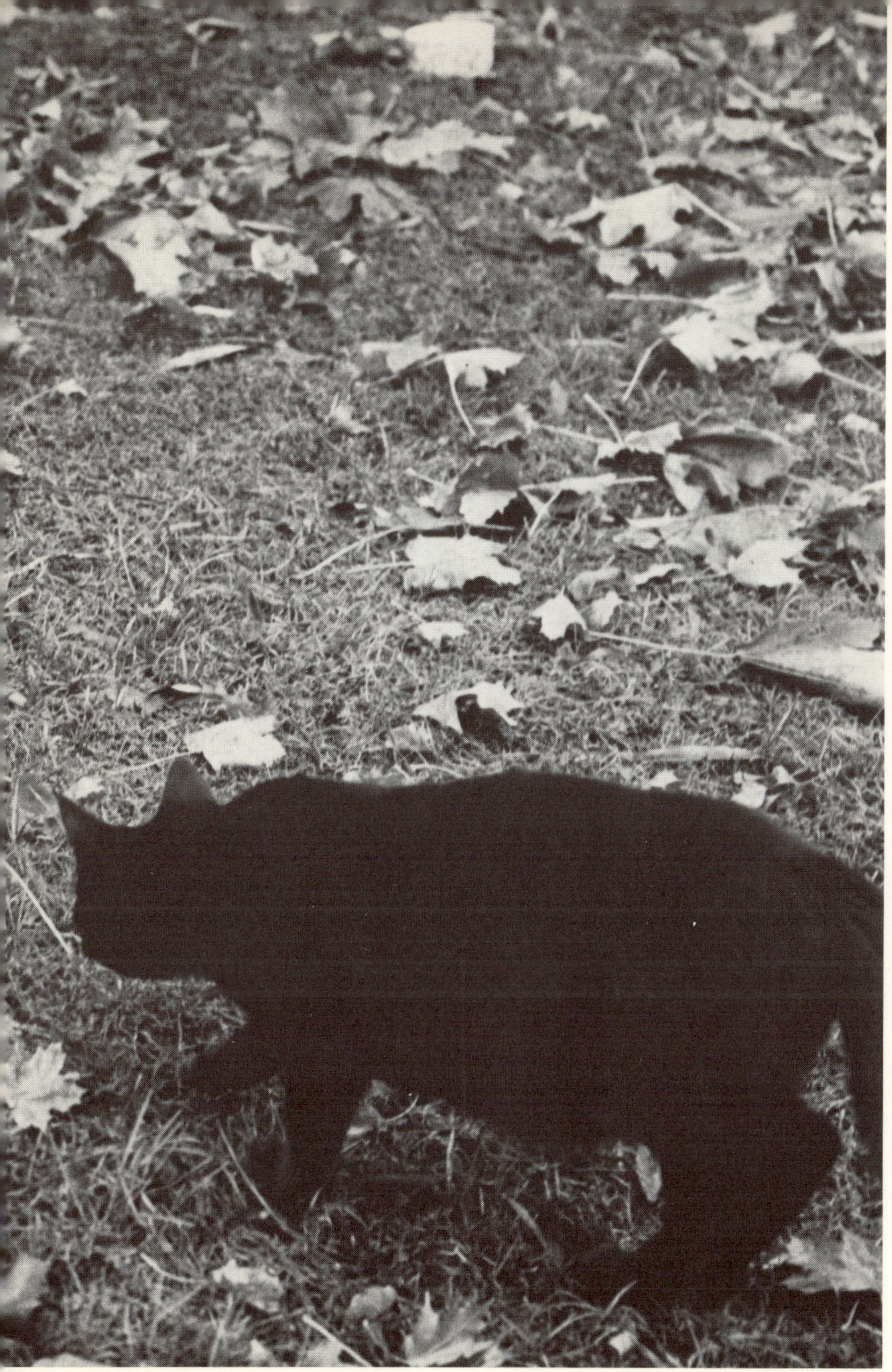

I've heard of low-income housing, but this is ridiculous!

Al Haig will do anything to get the President's attention.

Thanks so much for voting for my tax cut.

The Rose Garden hasn't looked the same since Jimmy and Rosalynn took the lawn mower back to Plains.

No matter what anyone says—it's a lonely life at the top.

At last—the country is in firm hands.

I'm really excited about going to Prince Charles's wedding.

Really, Nancy—that's how you are supposed to greet the Queen.

I think I found the last of the Nixon tapes.

Mr. President, we're Evans and Novak and our readers would like to know . . .

Look, Ronnie—I found some of your old pictures from Warner Brothers.

This one I've got to get for the Gipper.

I'd be honored to be the first woman on the Supreme Court.

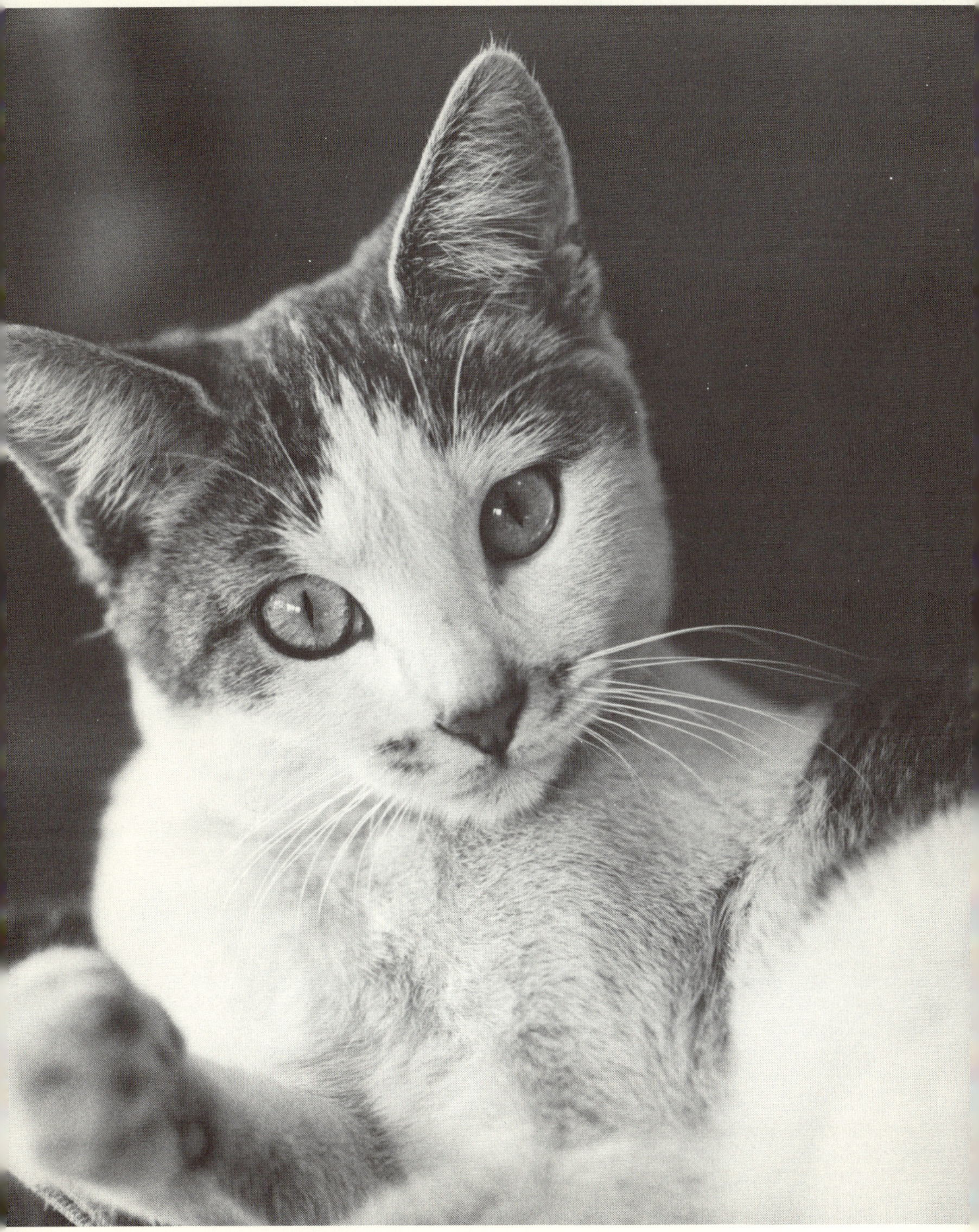

Mr. President, what are you doing for the little people?

The President just read another editorial in The Washington Post.

I always thought Air Force One left on time.

Tell Governor Brown I got another fruit fly.

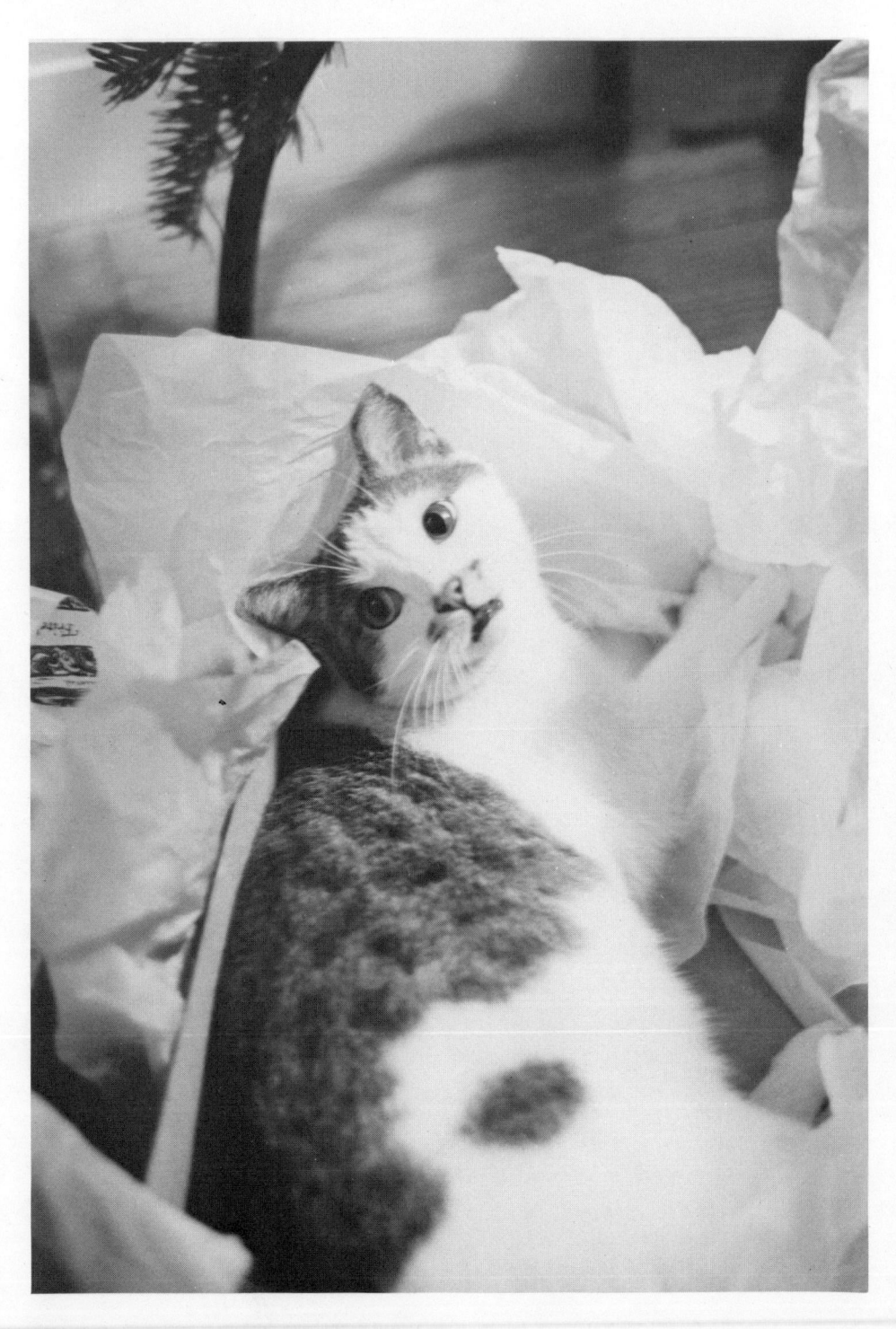

Oh, Ronnie! Not another surprise from Neiman-Marcus!

The President wants his TV set fixed before Dan Rather comes on!

Phyllis Schlafly has been in heaven since Ronnie became President.

I'm not leaving, Mr. President, until we balance the budget.

Another great speech, Ronnie.

Al Haig puts his foot in his mouth again.

I know we need Secret Service protection, but this is a little too much.

Ronnie, I'm going to have to recarpet the Red Room.

Next time we're only serving Perrier water at the White House dinner.

I'm the only one who really understands Reaganomics.

Nancy, can you keep a state secret?

I've checked, Ronnie. There aren't any jellybeans left.

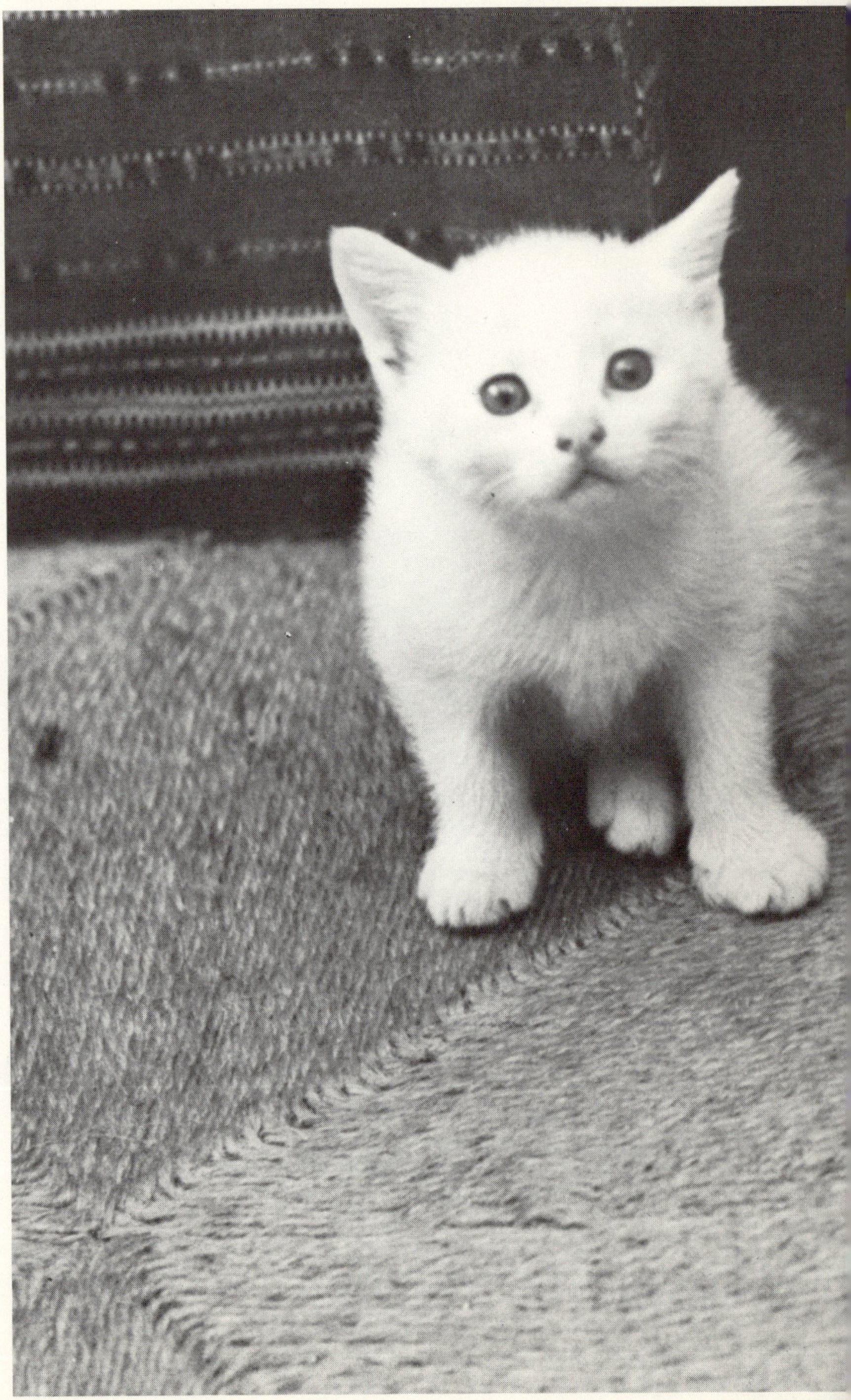

Even if it is a crisis, I'm not so sure we should wake the President.

I'm sorry, Mr. Kissinger, the President says you'll have to wait for an appointment.

There are times when I think maybe I should have taken the Pill.

The weekends at Camp David are great fun.

Mike Deaver is very close to the President.

Mr. President, I'd like to discuss the MX missile.

I believe in a full plate for white and black Americans.

Ted Kennedy said what?

Ronnie was never late for dinner when he was governor.

Wave to the crowd, Nancy. It's only three years to the next election.

I sleep better knowing he's in the White House.

Are you sure you know the way to the White House, Nancy?

I've never been happier since Ronnie became President.

This is the last of the federal handouts from this administration.

Barbara Walters is here for another interview.

The President says you can't come down until you vote for his defense budget.

Why do they keep writing those things about Nancy?

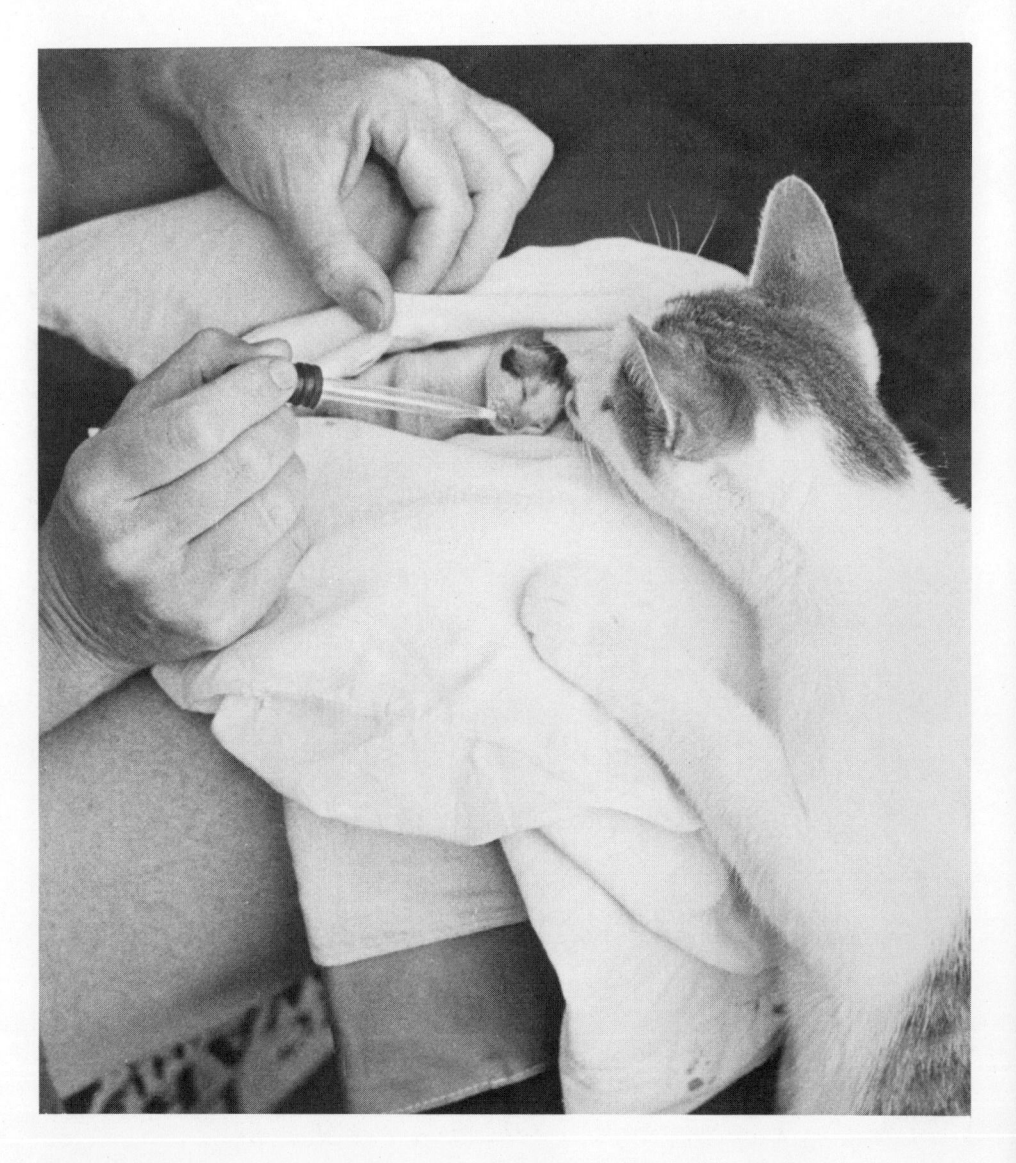

I'm really glad I supported the Right to Life movement.

Now let me see, where did I put the present for Jerry Falwell?

Redecorating the White House isn't as easy as I thought it would be.

Ronnie!

Nancy!

Ronnie, I don't have a thing to wear for the inauguration.

Why did I ever let Stockman cut my secretary out of the budget!

Someday we Democrats will have our own book.